Motherhood

A CELEBRATION

Also published by Carroll & Graf:

The Cosby Wit by Bill Adler

Motherhood

A CELEBRATION

BILL ADLER

Carroll & Graf Publishers, Inc.
New York

Carroll & Graf Publishers, Inc.
260 Fifth Avenue
New York, NY 10001

First printing 1987

Library of Congress Cataloging in Publication Data

Adler, Bill.
  Motherhood, a celebration.

  1. Mothers—Quotations, maxims, etc.   I. Title.
PN6084.M6A34   1987   082   87-739
ISBN: 0-88184-307-5

Manufactured in the United States of America

Motherhood
A Book of Quotations

Introduction

This book for and about mothers naturally contains a veritable garland of tributes to motherhood, and it is thus only appropriate that its official publication date should be Mother's Day. But while it is obviously a perfect gift to one's mother, a well-deserved salute to all she stands for, it is intended to be something more than that: a book to be dipped into again and again over the years, just for pleasure or as a source of reference for the perfect quote on a multitude of family occasions.

You will find many of the world's great writers and thinkers represented here, Plato and Sophocles, Shakespeare and Shaw, Tennyson and Dickens, as well as modern best-selling authors from John Updike to Danielle Steele and—of course—Erma Bombeck. Biblical quotations, the proverbs of many nations, and the lyrics to folk or popular songs old and new offer wisdom, sentiment and humor to delight the ear and the mind.

Motherhood is after all the great universal subject. As the Roman poet Lucretius put it, "The earth with good title has gotten and keeps the name of mother earth, since she of herself gave birth to mankind." Without mothers we would not be, and everyone has his or her thoughts on the special place that mothers occupy in our hearts and minds. Throughout this book you will find men and women of the greatest accomplishment, be it President John Quincy Adams, inventor Thomas Edison or poet Elizabeth Barrett Browning, paying tribute to their good fortune in having a mother who guided them towards the best in their natures.

Mothers themselves have their say, too, of course. They see their sons and daughters with an affectionate but clear eye, pleased but not overawed that a son has become President Jimmy Carter or a daughter a movie star called Cher. They speak of the joys and trials of pregnancy and birth, offer succinct advice on bringing up baby, and recall their mixed feelings on seeing their children move out into the world.

Whether it is the mother talking about the child, or the grown son or daughter celebrating the mother, you will find in this book words that will move you, make you reflect, at times astonish you, and often make you laugh out loud. Motherhood is a very serious calling, but it is also one inevitably fraught with humor. Mark Twain, Groucho Marx, Jean Kerr, Phyllis Diller and many others are here to remind you that motherhood can be a very funny business indeed.

The mother of tots or teenagers, the mother of grown children, the grandmother, and the young woman expecting her first child will all find their own feelings and experiences reflected here. And, not to limit ourselves, the curious husband, father or son cannot help but gain new insights into the sometimes mysterious world of mothers and motherhood. After all, every one of us is born of woman.

As an author, I expected the compiling of this book

to be a pleasure. But the riches—and the surprises—
were even greater than I expected. What fun to discover that Napoleon Bonaparte and Muhammad Ali
had extremely similar thoughts on the importance of
mothers to the spirit of the nation! How astonishing
that "Old Blood and Guts," General George S. Patton,
should have written an exceptionally poignant and
loving remembrance of his mother! How interesting
to know what a Tina Turner or a Meryl Streep regard
as the essence of motherhood! It was an adventure for
me, and I hope it will be one for you, too.

Bill Adler

Part I
A Mother Is

A mother is a mother still,
The holiest thing alive.
SAMUEL TAYLOR COLERIDGE

*G*od can't be always everywhere: and
so
Invented Mothers.

SIR EDWARD ARNOLD

*W*hen God thought of MOTHER, He must have laughed with satisfaction, and framed it quickly—so rich, so deep, so divine, so full of soul, power, and beauty, was the conception.

HENRY WARD BEECHER

*T*he mother in her office holds the key
Of the soul; and she it is who stamps the coin
Of character.

ANONYMOUS

*M*ost of all the beautiful things in life come by twos and threes, by dozens and hundreds. Plenty of roses, stars, sunsets, rainbows, brothers and sisters, aunts and cousins, but only one mother in the whole world.

KATE DOUGLAS WIGGIN

3

*M*ighty is the force of motherhood! It transforms all things by its vital heat.

GEORGE ELIOT

*S*trength and dignity are her clothing;
And she laugheth at the time to come.
She openeth her mouth with wisdom;
And the law of kindness is upon her tongue.
She looketh well to the ways of her household,
And eateth not the bread of idleness;
Her children rise up and call her blessed,
Her husband also and he praises her, saying,
  Many daughters have done virtuously,
  But thou excelleth them all.

PROVERBS 31:25–29

I am the poet of the woman the same as the man,
And I say it is as great to be a woman as to be a man,
And I say there is nothing greater than the mother
  of a man.

WALT WHITMAN

*T*he future destiny of the child is always the work of the mother. France needs nothing so much to promote her regeneration as good mothers.

NAPOLEON BONAPARTE

*T*he woman is the fiber of the nation. She is the producer of life. A nation is only as good as its women.

MUHAMMAD ALI

*I*nto the woman's keeping is committed the destiny of the generations to come after them.

THEODORE ROOSEVELT

*L*oved people are loving people.

ANN LANDERS

*M*other's love grows by giving.

CHARLES LAMB

*M*otherhood is, after all, woman's great and incomparable work.

EDWARD CARPENTER

*C*hildren are the anchors that hold a mother to life.

SOPHOCLES

*I*t must be said that the most important feature in a woman's history is her maternity.

FRANCES TROLLOPE

*T*he modest virgin, the prudent wife, or the careful matron, are much more serviceable in life than petticoated philsophers, blustering heroines, or virago queens. She who makes her husband and her children happy, who reclaims the one from vice, and trains the other up to virtue, is a much greater character than ladies described in romance, whose whole occupation is to murder mankind with shafts from the quiver of their eyes.

OLIVER GOLDSMITH

For a wife, take the daughter of a good mother.

THOMAS FULLER

The most important thing a father can do for his children is to love their mother.

REVEREND THEODORE HESBURGH

Where there is a mother in the house, matters speed well.

AMOS BRONSON ALCOTT

She could spot a hole in a sock a hundred miles away.

EDWARD KENNEDY, on his
mother, Rose Kennedy

As a little girl I had a very strong drive to be a mother. It's what I wanted more than anything else. I was very attached to my dolls—I had six of them—and I used to line them up in bed next to me. I was so busy making sure that they weren't going to be smothered that I couldn't sleep. . . .

I had to take very good care of my dolls. I knew my mother was doing it wrong, and I figured I could do it better.

BEATRICE SCHWARTZ

What can you say about a woman who was asked what it was like to be my mother and replied, "It's a rotten job, but someone had to do it?"

ERMA BOMBECK

$\mathcal{I}$t would seem that something which means poverty, disorder and violence every single day should be avoided entirely, but the desire to beget children is a natural urge.

PHYLLIS DILLER

$\mathcal{T}$he largeness of our mother-myth has a paradoxically dwindling effect upon the women concerned; they must be in all things motherly and become therefore natural processes rather than people. Few things are harder, in this era so preoccupied with the monitoring of human relations, than to get to know one's mother as a person—to forgive her, in effect, for being one's mother.

JOHN UPDIKE

$\mathcal{M}$others *are* and are not made.

GEORGE MIDDLETON

$\mathcal{H}$eaven help all mothers if they be not really dears.

SIR JAMES M. BARRIE

$\mathcal{M}$otherhood has a very humanizing effect. Everything gets reduced to essentials.

MERYL STREEP

$\mathcal{B}$ecause a young mother's welfare is of utmost concern to them, mothers-in-law, best friends, pediatricians, and psychiatrists are understandably hesitant about telling her what living with a young child is really like. The mothers-in-law tend to see it as asking the girl to shoot herself after she's already been hung. And the scientists, concerned as they are about overpopulation, quite naturally do not want to see things stop altogether.

BETTY CANARY

$\mathscr{L}$ord who ordainest for mankind
Benignant toils and tender cares
We thank thee for the ties that bind
The mother to the child she bears.

WILLIAM CULLEN BRYANT

$\mathcal{N}$o man is poor who has had a godly mother.

ABRAHAM LINCOLN

$\mathcal{M}$otherhood is the keystone of the arch of matrimonial happiness.

THOMAS JEFFERSON

$\mathcal{U}$nhappy is the man for whom his own mother has not made all other mothers venerable.

JEAN PAUL RICHTER

$\mathcal{T}$he earth with good title has gotten and keeps the name of mother earth, since she of herself gave birth to mankind.

LUCRETIUS

$\mathcal{W}$ho ever heard of Father Earth?

VANCE BOURJAILY

The harshness and general painfulness of life in old times must have been much relieved by certain simple and affectionate customs which modern people have learned to dispense with. Amongst these was a practice of going to see parents, and especially the female one, on the mid Sunday of Lent, taking for them some little present, such as a cake or trinket. A youth engaged in this amiable act of duty was said to go *a-mothering*, and thence the day itself came to be called Mothering Sunday.

CHAMBERS BOOK OF DAYS

Whereas the service rendered the United States by the American mother is the greatest source of the country's strength and admiration; and Whereas we honor ourselves and the mothers of America when we do any thing to give emphasis to the home as the fountain head of the State; and Whereas the American mother is doing so much for good government and humanity, we declare that the second Sunday of May will henceforth be celebrated as Mother's Day.

CONGRESSIONAL RESOLUTION, 1914

Mother's Day is a Day of Atonement in which formal restitution is made for the previous year's neglect.

GEOFFREY GORER

It's a mother's obligation, my mother used to say, to train children in the finer things of life, one of the finest being to remember their mother on Mother's Day.

TERESA BLOOMINGDALE

*E*very year I hear mothers complain that their children hardly notice Mother's Day; sometimes I wish I had that problem. At our house, we celebrate with a vengeance. To begin with, our seven children spend the entire day trying to be good, which is not only hard on them but hard on me, too. How long can you go on playing the Ideal Mommy?

SHIRLEY LUETH

*W*oman in the home has not yet lost her dignity, in spite of Mother's Day, with its offensive implication that our love needs an annual nudging, like our enthusiasm for the battle of Bunker Hill.

JOHN ERSKIN

I never thought you should be rewarded for the greatest privilege of life.

MARY ROPER COHEN, mother
of the year, 1958

*T*ake note of what men of old concluded:
That what there is shall go to those who are good
    for it,
Children to the motherly, that they shall prosper,
Carts to good drivers, that they be driven well,
The valley to the waterers, that it yield fruit.

BERTOLT BRECHT

PART II
Born of Woman

Although there are many trial marriages . . .
there is no such thing as a trial child.

GAIL SHEEHY

In the dark womb where I began
My mother's life made me a man.
Through all the months of human birth
Her beauty fed my common earth.

JOHN MASEFIELD

When we returned to Italy, my urge to be pregnant intensified. The actress part of me was happy and fulfilled, but the other half of me, the Neapolitan, child-bearing, Mother Earth half of me, was fiercely unsatisfied. At twenty-nine, I had become obsessive about turning thirty without having produced a child.

SOPHIA LOREN

In becoming pregnant, am I hoping to find a mother rather than become one?

PHYLLIS CHESLER

Of course, parents don't have children because they want to be martyrs, or at least they shouldn't. They have them because they love children and want some of their very own. They also love children because they remember being loved so much by their parents in their childhood. Taking care of their children, seeing them grow and develop into fine people, gives most parents—despite the hard work—their greatest satisfaction in life.

DR. BENJAMIN SPOCK

*W*omen's liberation is just a lot of foolishness. It's the men who are discriminated against. They can't bear children. And no one is likely to do anything about that.

GOLDA MEIR

A ship under sail, a man in complete armour, and a woman with a big belly are the three handsomest sights in the world.

JAMES HOWELL

M y dear angel has been qualmish of late, and begins to grow remarkably round in the waist.

TOBIAS SMOLLETT

I feel like a cow; I haven't gotten angry in weeks. I really am happy and contented. That satisfied smile must be driving some of my friends crazy with envy, or at least I hope it is. . . . For the first

time in my life, I have an excuse for being plump.
I am round and soft-looking. Yeah, no one expects
me to be sylphlike.

ANGELA BARRON MCBRIDE

I was also very affected by the first time I felt the
baby kick. And yet it wasn't a kick at all, which is
what I had been led to expect, but a flickering, like
a little butterfly alive in my belly.

SOPHIA LOREN

*T*here will be a singing in your heart
There will be a rapture in your eyes;
You will be a woman set apart,
You will be so wonderful and wise.

ROBERT W. SERVICE

*B*y far the most common craving of pregnant
women is not to be pregnant.

PHYLLIS DILLER

*D*uring the months of my pregnancy, I'd earned
well over a quarter of a million dollars, but would
definitely have preferred a gestation period of tran-
quility, and to be the hothouse for my child under
less trying circumstances.

JOAN FONTAINE

ℒong before she was born, I tried to influence her future life by association with music, art, and natural beauty. Perhaps this prenatal preparation helped make Shirley what she is today.

MRS. TEMPLE, Shirley's Mother

𝒲hen I had my baby last New Year's Day, it was quite an event, although not an entirely blessed one. I had a twenty-two hour labor, a near cesarean, a doctor who had an allergy attack from my perfume, and a big, big baby. They don't call it labor for nothing.

PIA ZADORA

𝒲hat's a mother for but to suffer?

ERMA BOMBECK

𝒜 funny thing happened to my mother one day—me.

JACK PARR

𝒥t was daybreak, Thursday, August 27, 1908, on the Sam Johnson farm on the Pedernales River, near Stonewall, Gillespie County. In the rambling old farmhouse of the young Sam Johnsons, lamps had burned all night. Now the light came in from the east, bringing a deep stillness, a stillness so profound and pervasive that it seemed as if the earth itself were listening. And then there came a sharp compelling cry—the most awesome, happiest sound known to human ears—the cry of a

newborn baby; the first child of Sam and Rebekah
Johnson was "discovering America."

REBEKAH BAINES JOHNSON, describing

the birth of her son Lyndon

*D*id you ever see a very young baby? The first
days or weeks they are so unhappy. They seem to
resent being brought into this world. They cry a
great deal. Some of them have little, old wrinkled
faces. When I looked at Mary, I felt like apologiz-
ing to her for bringing her into a world that,
manifestly, she did not like. I shall always remember that and never in any circumstances prate
about what she owes me. I owe her all the care I
can give for bringing her into a world she did not
seem to want to live in.

HELEN HAYES

*T*here is an amazed curiosity in every young
mother. It is strangely miraculous to see and to
hold a living being formed within oneself and
issued forth from oneself.

SIMONE DE BEAUVOIR

*T*he merest grin of maternal beatitude
Is worth a world of dull virginity.

GERALD GOULD

*I*s not a young mother one of the sweetest sights
life shows us?

WILLIAM MAKEPEACE THACKERY

The moment a child is born,
the mother is also born.
She never existed before.
The woman existed, but the mother, never.
A mother is something absolutely new.

RAJNEESH

Now the thing about having a baby—and I can't be the first person to have noticed this—is that thereafter you have it.

JEAN KERR

As soon as I stepped out of my mother's womb on to dry land, I realized that I had made a mistake—that I shouldn't have come, but the trouble with children is that they are not returnable.

QUENTIN CRISP

Mothers are fonder of their children than fathers, for they remember the pain of bringing them forth, and are surer that they are their own.

ARISTOTLE

Mother is the name for God in the lips and hearts of little children.

WILLIAM MAKEPEACE THACKERY

The mother's face and voice are the first conscious objects the infant soul unfolds, and she soon comes to stand in the very place of God to her child.

GRANVILLE STANLEY HALL

He hungered; and she gave
What most His heart did crave,
A Mother's love.

JOHN BANNISTER TABB

. . . blest the babe,
Nursed in his Mother's arms, who sucks to sleep
Rocked on his Mother's breast, who with his soul
Drinks in the feelings of his Mother's eye!

WILLIAM WORDSWORTH

Mother's arms are made of tenderness, and sweet
sleep blesses the child who lies therein.

VICTOR HUGO

What tigress is there that does not purr over her
young ones, and fawn upon them in tenderness?

ST. AUGUSTINE

I love the cradle songs the mothers sing
In lonely places where the twilight drops
The slow endearing melodies that bring
Sleep to the weeping lids.

FRANCIS LEDWIDGE

How sweet are the thoughts that fill my heart
Today, dear mother of mine!
Memories that stand in the mist of the years,
Fadeless, enduring forever;

The comfort of your arms—my first cradle;
The solace of your voice—my first music;
The caress of your hands—my first shelter;
The touch of your lips—my first message of love.

PHILIP E. GREGORY

B eat upon mine, little heart! beat, beat!
Beat upon mine! you are mine, my sweet!
All mine from your pretty blue eyes to your feet,
    My sweet!

ALFRED, LORD TENNYSON

I t is safer in a mother's lap than in a lord's bed.

ESTONIAN PROVERB

O ver my slumbers your loving watch keep;
Rock me to sleep, mother, rock me to sleep.

ELIZABETH CHASE

T hey say that man is mighty,
    He governs land and sea,
He wields a mighty scepter
    O'er lesser powers that be;
But a mightier power and stronger
    Man from his throne has hurled,
For the hand that rocks the cradle
    Is the hand that rules the world.

WILLIAM ROSS WALLACE

"*T* he hand that rocks the cradle"—but today there's
    no such hand.

It is bad to rock the baby, they would have us
  understand;
So the cradle's but a relic of the former foolish
  days,
When mothers reared their children in unscien-
  tific ways;
When they jounced them and they bounced them,
  those poor dwarfs of long ago—
The Washingtons and Jeffersons and Adamses,
  you know.

attributed to BISHOP CROSWELL DOANE

*C*hildren are what the mothers are,
No fondest father's care
Can fashion so the infant heart
As those creative beams that dart,
With all their hopes and fears, upon
The cradle of a sleeping son.

WALTER SAVAGE LANDOR

*F*ull swells the deep pure fountain of young life
Where *on* the heart and *from* the heart we took
Our first and sweetest nurture, when the wife,
Blest into mother, in the innocent look,
Or even the piping cry of lips that brook
No pains and small suspense, a joy perceives
Man knows not, when from out its cradled nook,
She sees her little bud put forth its leaves.

LORD BYRON

B egin, baby boy, to recognize your mother with a smile.

VIRGIL

"*Y* ou agreed to get up nights."
    This is true. I stumble into the nursery, pick up my son, so small, so perfect, and as he fastens himself to me like a tiny, sucking minnow I am flooded with tenderness.

SARA DAVIDSON

L ike snowmen, babies have no proper necks, but there is a place right behind the ears and down an inch where head meets torso that is heaven to nuzzle. Babies have delicate hands and lie with palms opened, and you'd be astounded how much time a grown woman can waste watching her infant rearrange his fingers.

TERRY HEKKER

M y mother's hands are cool and fair,
    They can do anything.
Delicate mercies hide them there
    Like flowers in the spring.

ANNA HEMPSTEAD BRANCH

C an a mother sit and hear
    An infant groan, an infant fear?
No, no! never can it be!
Never, never can it be!

WILLIAM BLAKE

$\mathcal{D}$o you perhaps think that nature gave woman nipples as a kind of beauty spot, not for the purpose of nourishing their children?

FAVORINUS

$\mathcal{W}$hat art can a woman be good at? Oh, vain!
What art *is* she good at, but hurting her breast
With the milk-teeth of babes, and a smile at the pain?

ELIZABETH BARRETT BROWNING

$\mathcal{W}$omanliness means only motherhood;
All love begins and ends there—roams enough,
But, having run the circle, rests at home.

ROBERT BROWNING

$\mathcal{M}$other and child—think of it my friends, on Christmas day. What more beautiful sight is there in the world? What more beautiful sight, and what more wonderful sight?

What more beautiful? That man must be very far from the kingdom of God—he is not worthy to be called a man at all—whose heart has not been touched by the sight of his first child in its mother's bosom.

WALTER KINGSLEY

$\mathcal{T}$he bearing and training of a child
Is woman's wisdom.

ALFRED, LORD TENNYSON

𝒜nother thing that has not changed is children's earliest needs. They learn about the world not merely *from* their mothers, but *through* them: through the emotional ties which show them what feeling is, what connection is, what response is. Babies learn love and trust and their place in the universe from the people who look after them first, and this learning is the foundation and the shaping plan for everything that happens after that. So it has been, and so it is.

ELIZABETH JANEWAY

𝒯he only time a woman really succeeds in changing a man is when he is a baby.

NATALIE WOOD

𝒥f you doubt that the child shows the man, consider this: eighteen-month-old Cassius Clay (now Muhammad Ali) was being cuddled on Mummy's lap one day when a tiny fist shot straight up and knocked out one of Mummy's teeth.

HARRIET VAN HORNE

𝒯hey say there is no other
Can take the place of mother.
GEORGE BERNARD SHAW

𝒮imply having children does not make mothers.

JOHN A. SHEDD

A lot of people assume that because I am the mother of ten children I must be an expert on motherhood, but such is not the case. It is true that I have learned a great deal over the years, but fortunately I have managed to forget most of what I have learned. (That is how I stayed sane.)

TERESA BLOOMINGDALE

Men resent women because women bear kids, and seem to have this magic link with immortality that men lack. But they should stay home for a day with a kid; they'd change their minds.

TUESDAY WELD

Total immersion in vitamin drops and baby blankets does things to a woman. Although she seldom notices it, she is garnering stares at the supermarket because of her linty-woolly appearance. She sometimes elicits loud guffaws from bystanders—particularly if, at a company banquet, she turns to her husband and without blinking an eye asks, "Is its din-din good?"

BETTY CANARY

I remember a time when I marched into Katherine Josephine's room and pretended to be surprised to discover that somebody was occupying the bassinet. "Don't tell me that *you're* still here!" I exclaimed. "Listen, kid, do you know what day it is? It's the ninth, you're four months old, and you're not getting any younger, let me tell you.

These are your best months and what are you doing with them? Nothing. For your information, babies a lot smaller than you are already out advertising North Star Blankets and you just lie here fluttering your fingers."

JEAN KERR

*W*ho ran to help me when I fell
And would some pretty story tell,
Or kiss the place to make it well?
My mother.

ANN TAYLOR

A toddler, according to the dictionary, is one who toddles, which means "to walk with short tottering steps. . . ." Regardless of what the experts or the outsiders say, those tiny steps will plunge you into one of the most exasperating periods of your adult life.

JAIN SHERRARD

*P*erhaps a better woman after all,
With chubby children hanging on my neck
To keep me low and wise.

ELIZABETH BARRETT BROWNING

*H*e that wipes the child's nose kisseth the mother's cheek.

GEORGE HERBERT

When people inquire, I always just state,
I have four nice children and hope to have eight.

ALINE KILMER

Being a full-time mother is one of the highest
salaried jobs in my field, since the payment is
pure love.

MILDRED B. VERMONT

There was a place in childhood, that I remember
  well,
And there a voice of sweetest tone, bright fairy
  tales did tell,
And gentle words, and fond embrace, were given
  with joy to me,
When I was in that happy place upon my mother's knee.

SAMUEL LOVER

Before a day was over,
Here comes the rover,
For his mother's kiss—sweeter this
Than any other thing!

WILLIAM ALLINGHAM

My sole consolation when I went upstairs for the
night was that Momma would come in and kiss
me after I was in bed.

MARCEL PROUST

Mother tells me "Happy Dreams!" and takes
    away the light,
An' leaves me lying all alone an' seein'
    things at night.

                                   EUGENE FIELD

Now in memory comes my mother,
    As she used to in years agone,
To regard the darling dreamers
    Eere she left them till the dawn.

                             COATES KINNEY

I have so many anxieties about her growing up. I
just hope she will get a chance to grow up. I hope
there's a world for her to grow up in. I watch the
news and I think, "God damn these guys' they're
going to blow up the world, just when I've got
this little peach here."

                             MERYL STREEP

The years rush past, as every older woman will
tell the young mothers who complain that they
still have two little ones at home and it seems like
forever before they will *all* be in school. Oh no,
they say—time flies—enjoy them while they're
young—they grow up so fast. . . .

    The mothers agree that indeed the years do fly.
It's the days that don't. The hours, minutes of a
single day sometimes just stop. And a mother

finds herself standing in the middle of a room wondering. Wondering. Years fly. Of course they do. But a mother can gag on a day.

JAIN SHERRARD

𝒜 nd there is the mixed consolation of knowing that one day, in the not distant future, my stint of full-time motherhood will end. Yesterday morning after our weekly visit to the library, my daughter, now two and a half, spotted a group of three-and-four-year-olds lining up outside the building across the street and asked to follow them. Kate has been talking of nothing but nursery school ever since. Already I miss her.

BARBARA HUSTEDT CROOK

PART III
Bringing Up Baby

My mother had a great deal of trouble with me but I think she enjoyed it.

SAMUEL CLEMENS (MARK TWAIN)

$\mathcal{C}$ asier it is to rule a band of savages than to the successful autocrat of thy little kingdom.

JOHN HABBERTON

$\mathcal{I}$f you bungle raising your children, I don't think whatever else you do matters very much.

JACQUELINE KENNEDY ONASSIS

$\mathcal{W}$omen know
The way to rear up children (to be just),
They know a simple, merry, tender knack
Of tying sashes, fitty baby-shoes,
And stringing pretty words that make no sense,
And kissing full senses into empty words;
Which things are corals to cut life upon,
Although such trifles.

ELIZABETH BARRETT BROWNING

$\mathcal{S}$poil your husband, but don't spoil your children.

LOUISE SEVIER GIDDINGS CURREY,
Mother of the Year, 1961

People have asked me if I ever spanked Jack when he was a boy. I suppose it is part of the mystique surrounding the presidency that anyone who occupies the office is endowed with qualities that are extraordinary and he must have passed through childhood in a glow of virtue. I can state that this was not the case with Jack, nor was it with Bobby or Teddy or any of the others, and whenever they needed it they got a good old-fashioned spanking, which I believe is one of the most effective means of instruction.

ROSE KENNEDY

The mother's heart is the child's schoolroom.

HENRY WARD BEECHER

But a mother is like a broomstick or the sun in the heavens, it does not matter which as far as one's knowledge of her is concerned: the broomstick is there and the sun is there; and whether the child is beaten by it or warmed and enlightened by it, it accepts it as a fact in nature, and does not conceive it as having had youth, passions, and weaknesses, or as still growing, yearning, suffering, and learning.

GEORGE BERNARD SHAW

Being a housewife and a mother is the biggest job in the world, but if it doesn't interest you, don't do it. . . . I would have made a terrible parent. The first time my child didn't do what I wanted, I'd kill him.

KATHARINE HEPBURN

*T*he thing that impresses me most about America is the way parents obey their children.

EDWARD, DUKE OF WINDSOR

*T*he easiest way to convince my children that they don't need anything is to get it for them.

JOAN COLLINS

I am more and more impressed with the responsibility of training children properly. I find that Willie needs constant watching and correcting, and it requires great concentration and firmness to do the right thing always. It seems to me that there is no stronger motive for improvement than the thought of the influence on our children. It is what we *are*, not what we do in reference to them, which will make its impress on their lives. They will be sure to find out our weak points whatever professions we make.

LOUISA TORREY TAFT, mother
of William Howard Taft

*N*oel loved to look after me when he was a boy, he was so capable that I depended on him perhaps more than I should, when he was so young. He always knew the right thing to do, his opinion was really law to me, for he was always right.

VIOLET VEITCH COWARD, mother
of Noel Coward

James James
Morrison Morrison
Weatherby George Dupree
Took great
Care of his Mother
Though he was only three.
James James
Said to his Mother,
"Mother," he said, said he:
"You must never go down to the end of the town,
If you don't go down with me."

A.A. MILNE

A suburban mother's role is to deliver children obstetrically once, and by car forever after.

PETER DE VRIES

Everyone knows what a mother is.

A mother is someone who makes you wear galoshes when it isn't raining. She gives you aspirin when you have a cold and reads you stories before bed.

A mother is a happy, warm, patient person who effortlessly maintains a beautiful, spotless home. She plays games with her children joyously, teaches them constantly, and takes them to the doctor, the dentist, the zoo, the park, swimming and camping—sometimes all on the same day.

SHIRLEY RADL

One of my children wrote in a third grade piece on how her mother spent her time. She reported, "one half time on home, one half time on outside things, one half time writing." An exact description of how it seemed to me, too.

CHARLOTTE MONTGOMERY

Most children threaten at times to run away from home. This is the only thing that keeps some parents going.

PHYLLIS DILLER

God knows that a mother needs fortitude and courage and tolerance and flexibility and patience and firmness and nearly every other brave aspect of the human soul. But because I happen to be a parent of almost fiercely maternal nature, I praise *casualness*. It seems to me the rarest of virtues. It is useful enough when children are small. It is important to the point of necessity when they are adolescents.

PHILLIS MCGINLEY

Adolescence is that period in a kid's life when his or her parents become more difficult.

RYAN O'NEAL

𝒩othing can compare in beauty, and wonder, and admirableness, and divinity itself, to the silent work in obscure dwellings of faithful women bringing their children to honour and virtue and piety.

HENRY WARD BEECHER

𝒢ive me the life of the boy whose mother is nurse, seamstress, washerwoman, cook, teacher, angel, and saint, all in one, and whose father is guide, exemplar, and friend. No servants to come between. These are the boys who are born to the best fortune.

ANDREW CARNEGIE

𝐼 hated the servants and liked my mother because, on the one or two rare and delightful occasions when she buttered my bread for me, she buttered it thickly instead of merely wiping a knife on it.

GEORGE BERNARD SHAW

𝑀y mother made a brilliant impression upon my childhood life. She shone for me like the evening star—I loved her dearly, but at a distance.

WINSTON CHURCHILL

𝒯he mother loves her child most divinely, not when she surrounds him with comfort and anticipates his wants, but when she resolutely holds him to the highest standards and is content with nothing less than his best.

HAMILTON WRIGHT MABIE

God made mothers before He made ministers: the progress of Christ's kingdom depends more upon the influence of faithful, wise and pious mothers than upon any other human agency.

T. L. CUYLER

An ounce of mother is worth a pound of clergy.

SPANISH PROVERB

One good mother is worth a hundred schoolmasters.

GEORGE HERBERT

Do you expect, forsooth, that a mother will hand down to her children principles which differ from her own?

JUVENAL

And high above all memories
I hold the beauty of her mind.

FREDERICK HENTZ ADAMS

She faced the world with level blue eyes, filled with the love of love, the hate of tyranny and wrong, the recognition of whatever beauty—and there was all too little of it—came within her vision.

HERBERT QUICK

If you would reform the world from its errors and vices, begin by enlisting the mothers.

CHARLES SIMMONS

$\mathcal{M}$y mother took for her motto in the training of her children the saying of some distinguished man: "Fill the measure with wheat and there will be no room for the chaff."

MARIA SANFORD

$\mathcal{I}$n the eyes of its mother every beetle is a gazelle.

MOROCCAN PROVERB

$\mathcal{M}$others soften their children with kisses and imperfect noises, with the pap and breastmilk of soft endearments; they rescue them from tutors, and snatch them from discipline. They desire to keep them fat and warm and their feet dry, and their bellies full, and then the children govern, and cry, and prove fools and troublesome.

JEREMY TAYLOR

$\mathcal{A}$ child may have too much of his mother's blessing.

ENGLISH PROVERB

$\mathcal{A}$ spoilt child never loves its mother.

SIR HENRY TAYLOR

$\mathcal{I}$f I had another child—I'd like a girl—I can't say just how I'd raise her, but one thing I can tell you is that she will not be spoiled. The whole thing is about earning your own way and you don't really get there until you earn it. That's the real truth.

TINA TURNER

A father is proud of those sons who have merit, and puts the rest lower. But a mother, though she is proud of the former too, cherishes most the latter.

CONFUCIUS

A mother's love and a mother's prayers may indeed follow their object around the world; but the personal intercourse and daily contact between mother and son have a sacramental virtue in guarding and shaping a boy's course such as nothing else on earth can supply.

G. W. E. RUSSELL

No one can misunderstand a boy like his own mother.

NORMAN DOUGLAS

There is a harmony and beauty in the life of mother and son that brims the mind's cup of satisfaction.

CHRISTOPHER MORLEY

For the entire five years of my son's life, I have been preparing him to worship the ground I walk on. To date, my crusade hasn't even gotten him to bended knee.

CLAUDETTE RUSSEL

My mother loved children. She would have given anything if I'd been one.

GROUCHO MARX

*W*ith what price we pay for the glory of motherhood.

ISADORA DUNCAN

*B*eing constantly with children was like wearing a pair of shoes that were expensive and too small. She couldn't bear to throw them out, but they gave her feet blisters.

BERYL BAINBRIDGE

*T*o be a good housewife and mother, you have to be more self-generated. You have to create your own playground of the imagination, and the mind. To be a really good, creative mother you have to be an extraordinary woman. You have to keep yourself involved with your child during great periods of the day when it's just the two of you and you feel that at any moment you may literally go out of your mind.

MERYL STREEP

*Y*es, a mother is one thing that nobody can do without. And when you have harassed her, buffeted her about, tried her patience, and worn her out, and it seems that the end of the world is about to descend upon you, then you can win her back with four little words. "Mom, I love you!"

WILLIAM A. GREENBAUM II

*C*hildren reflect constant cares, but uncertain comforts.

RICHARD BRATHWAITE

Motherhood is *not* for the fainthearted. Used frogs, skinned knees, and the insults of teenage girls are not meant for the wimpy.

DANIELLE STEELE

Even a child is known by his doings.

PROVERBS 20:11

When children are doing nothing, they are doing mischief.

HENRY FIELDING

A rascal of a child—that age is without pity.

LA FONTAINE

Let thy child's first lesson be obedience, and the second will be what thou wilt.

BENJAMIN FRANKLIN

Children are to be won to follow liberal studies by exhortations and rational motives and on no account be forced thereto by whipping.

PLUTARCH

Spare the rod and spoil the child.

SAMUEL BUTLER

Speak roughly to your little boy,
　And beat him when he sneezes:
He only does it to annoy,
　Because he knows it teases.

LEWIS CARROLL

$\mathcal{I}$t is better to bind your children to you by respect and gentleness, than by fear.

TERRENCE

$\mathcal{C}$hildren have more need of models than of critics.

JOUBERT

$\mathcal{I}$ think a parent is always tougher on a child of the same sex—because they're *us*. Vanessa is exactly me: stubborn, independent-minded, emotional, quixotic, moody—and lacking in confidence.

JANE FONDA

$\mathcal{J}$ust as the twig is bent the tree's inclined.

ALEXANDER POPE

$\mathcal{T}$rain up a child in the way that he should go; and when he is old, he will not depart from it.

PROVERBS 22:6

$\mathcal{P}$arents learn a lot from their children about coping with life.

MURIEL SPARK

$\mathcal{W}$atching Clementine grow is one of the great satisfactions of my life. The center of the universe shifting from myself to another person is a great relief. It gives me the chance to give to another person. I'm not so concerned about my own life as I was before.

CYBIL SHEPHERD

ℐ think it must somewhere be written, that the virtues of mothers shall be visited on their children, as well as the sins of their fathers.

CHARLES DICKENS

𝒯he father's always a Republican toward his son, and the mother's always a Democrat.

ROBERT FROST

𝒯he other day I said to her, "All children rebel, and I *know* you're going to go against us. You'll probably go to college and become a right-wing conservative Republican!" And she looked at me and said, "Mother, I may well become a conservative Republican, but if I do, it won't be because I have to rebel against you. Don't be so arrogant as to assume everything I do is because of *you*."

JANE FONDA

𝒪h what a tangled web do parents weave
When they think that their children are naive.

OGDEN NASH

ℳy own mother, whom I still regard with awe and, at times, downright disbelief, best illustrates the stone-blind approach to motherhood. She constantly and without blushing referred to her three daughters as "my three jewels." She wasn't a liar, understand. She merely seemed totally obvlivious to the facts. My father naturally referred to us no more than was absolutely necessary and, if memory serves me right, when he did refer to us, he usually prefaced his remarks with, "For God's sake!"

BETTY CANARY

𝒮he has no name. Her phone number is unlisted. But she exists in the mind of every child who has ever tried to get his own way and used her as a last resort.

Everybody else's mother is right out of the pages of Greek mythology—mysterious, obscure, and surrounded by hearsay.

She is the answer to every child's prayer.

Traditional Mother: "Have the car home by eleven or you're grounded for a month."

Everybody Else's Mother: "Come home when you feel like it."

ERMA BOMBECK

𝓜y kids see me as a person, and there's a lot of respect on both sides. They're not afraid of my ups and downs the way I was afraid to see my mother's or my father's. My kids and I are friends, and, even though I have tried to give them values, I'm not a dictator. I don't set impossible standards. If one of them felt rebellious and said he wanted to spray-paint his hair green, I'd say great, that's fine, spray your hair green.

I may be eating these words in a year or so, but I think kids need to experience things their own way.

SALLY FIELD

𝒮ome people used to say that Dad had so many children he couldn't keep track of them. Dad himself used to tell a story about one time when Mother went off to fill a lecture engagement and left him in charge at home. When Mother returned, she asked him if everything had run smoothly.

"Didn't have any trouble except with that one over there," he replied. "But a spanking brought him into line."

Mother could handle any crisis without losing her composure.

"That's not one of ours, dear," she said. "He belongs next door."

FRANK B. GILBRETH, JR., and
ERNESTINE GILBRETH CAREY

𝒲hat I think I have in common with every mother on the face of the earth is the primacy of one's children in one's life—that they're everything in some bizarre way.

JANE SILVERMAN

𝒥t's as if I'm two people: mother enjoys the present moment; MOTHER is constantly reminding, admonishing, worrying, forecasting. One is a person, the other an instutition. . . .

ANGELA BARRAN MCBRIDE

𝒥or the mother is and must be, whether she knows it or not, the greatest, strongest and most lasting teacher her children have.

HANNAH WHITALL SMITH

𝒯he crying need of the world is mental mothers. Primitive, physical, passionate mothers we have in abundance. But the mothers we need, the mothers who are to stimulate mentally the town, family, and church are all too rare.

FRANK R. ARNOLD

𝒴ou may have tangible wealth untold,
Caskets of jewels and coffers of gold.
Richer than I you can never be—
I had a mother who read to me.

STRICKLAND GILLIAN

𝑀y mother usually somehow managed, at eleven, to sit down in the red rocking chair by the window . . . and allow us to sit upon our red stools while, our cookies and milk consumed, she herself would read aloud to us. Here was the very doorsill to complete enchantment, for she was as seemingly as lost as we in whatever she was reading. The iron teakettle simmered on The Rising Sun; the red geraniums glowed with life; smells of our approaching dinner filled our noses from stewpans or baking dishes; while my mother's voice brought trooping into our kitchen all those with whom we rejoiced or suffered, admired or feared, loved or hated.

MARY ELLEN CHASE

𝒥riday. Rain. The end of school. He could stay home . . . and do nothing, stay near his mother the whole afternoon. He turned from the table and regarded her. She was seated before the table paring beets. . . . Above her blue and white checkered apron, her face bent down, intent upon her work, her lips pressed gravely together. He loved her. He was happy again.

HENRY ROTH

𝑀y mother insisted I make my own decisions and live by them. I remember even when I was very young she would take me to the store to choose the material for a dress. I had to choose the material. But afterward I also had to wear the dress.

CHASE GOING WOODHOUSE

𝑀y mom buys things I wouldn't wear in a million years.

CHASTITY BONO, daughter of Cher

𝒲hen I try to pull "mother" from my childhood memories, I come up with two images, both of them, I fear, embodied in some work of fiction or another. In one, my mother, young and rather formally dressed, is sitting opposite me on the floor, coloring at the same page of a coloring book. I marvel at how neatly she does it, even though, from her vantage the page is upside down. She seems calm and comely and I am so proud it makes me shy. In the other, we are both somewhat older, and I see her, while standing at the ironing board, jump slightly and touch her jaw with her hand: a twinge of toothache, and my first unsolicited empathy into the pain of another human being.

JOHN UPDIKE

*B*ut I was in love with my mother, too. I hated her doing housework, could not bear the sight of her in an old dress and a pair of unlaced ox-fords, feeding soapy bed sheets into the wringer, scraping carrots and parsnips at the sink. But one thing she had acquired in town was the ability to be glamorous, to divorce herself, by means of paints and polishes, from the other world. I loved her glamorous aspect.

She had a wonderful drawer full of cosmet-ics. . . . Not every day, but once a week, or any time she was going out shopping, she would bathe, put on her stockings and a lacy slip and high-heeled shoes, and sit down to paint. I would abandon dog, swing, book, or any other pursuit in order to watch her.

SHIRLEY ABBOT

*S*he had the world's most beautiful speaking voice. As I am not a musician, I can only say her singing voice was melodious and well phrased, and as a child I was in heaven when her soprano notes in "A Little Brown Bird Singing" or "Who Is Syl-via? What Is She?" would come floating up the stairs to my sickroom. Her diction, her choice of words, the timbre of her voice could make angels weep with jealousy.

JOAN FONTAINE

*A*nd when she spake,
Sweet words, like dropping honey, she did shed;
And 'twixt the pearls and rubies, softly brake
A silver sound that heavenly music seem'd to make.

EDMUND SPENSER

*M*y mother taught older children to play the piano. It was a large black piano which took up half the space in our front room, and on late afternoons when it began to get dark, I would sit in my room and listen to the music from the front. It was not the music they played over and over, up and down the scale, that I liked, but the things my mother would play when she told the children, "Now *I'll* play your piece all the way through like Mr. Mozart would want it played." I can sometimes hear her music now, after thirty years—and remember the leaves falling on some smoky autumn afternoon, the air crisp and the sounds of dogs barking and train whistles far away.

WILLIE MORRIS

PART IV
Out Into The World

No man is really old until his mother stops worrying about him.

PROVERB

A mother's hardest to forgive.
Life is the fruit she longs to hand you,
Ripe on a plate. And while you live
Relentlessly she understands you.

PHYLLIS MCGINLEY

t he worst to be said
about mothers
is that they
are prone
to give
kisses
of con-
grat-
u-
lation
which make you feel
like a battleship
on which someone
is breaking
a bottle.

NORMAN MAILER

*F*or me, a line from mother is more efficacious than all the homilies preached in Lent.

HENRY WADSWORTH LONGFELLOW

*M*y mother's chastening love I own.

JOHN GREENLEAF WHITTIER

*T*here is more to being a Jewish mother than being Jewish and a mother. (On the other hand, you don't have to be either Jewish or a mother to be a Jewish mother. An Irish waitress or an Italian barber could also be a Jewish mother.) Properly practiced, Jewish motherhood is an art—a complex network of subtle and highly sophisticated techniques.

Master these techniques and you will be an unqualified success—the envy of your friends and the backbone of your family.

Fail to master these techniques and you hasten the black day you discover your children can get along without you.

DAN GREENBURG

*Y*ou never know how you were as a parent until your child grows up.

PRISCILLA PRESLEY

*M*others of daughters are daughters of mothers and have remained so, in circles joined to circles, since time began.

SIGNE HAMMER

*A*nybody without a child, or anybody without *your* child, will be very happy to calmly look at you and say: "The kid will be all right. The kid will be all right." But as a parent, you keep saying, "No, the kid won't. That's why I've got to stay on him. I've got to make sure. I've got to check." That's why mothers get up in the middle of the night and call a thirty-five-year-old son or a thirty-five-year-old daughter.

BILL COSBY

*W*hat the daughter does, the mother did.

JEWISH PROVERB

*A*ll women become like their mothers. That is their tragedy. No man does. That's his.

OSCAR WILDE

A fluent tongue is the only thing a mother doesn't like her daughter to resemble her in.

RICHARD BRINSLEY SHERIDAN

*M*y wife is the kind of girl who'll not go anywhere without her mother, and her mother will go anywhere.

JOHN BARRYMORE

I seem to be the victim of a cruel jest
It all concerns the person that I love best
She's just the dearest thing that I have ever known
Somehow we never get a chance to be alone.

My car will meet her, and her mother comes too.
It's a two-seater; still her mother comes too.
And when they're visiting me, we finish afternoon tea
She likes to sit on my knee—and her mother does,
too.

IVOR NOVELLO

$\mathcal{D}$on't tell my mother I'm living in sin.

A. P. HERBERT

$\mathcal{I}$ am going to New York to live with a married
ballerina who is ten years older than I am. P.S. I
am a Buddhist.

PATRICK DUFFY, in a note
home to his parents

"$\mathcal{L}$ike mother, like son," is the saying so true,
The world will judge largely of "mother" by you.

MARGARET JOHNSTON GRIFFIN

$\mathcal{T}$he mother's yearning, that completest type of life
within another life which is the essence of human
love, feels the presence of the cherished child even
in the base degraded man.

GEORGE ELIOT

$\mathcal{F}$or one on the ocean of crime long tossed,
Who loves his mother, is not quite lost.

THOMAS DUNN ENGLISH

If I took a tommy gun and shot up hundreds of people in a shopping mall, [my mother] would say, "They must have said something truly awful to him."

NORMAN MAILER

Who is it that loves me and will love me forever with an affection which no chance, no misery, no crime of mine can do away?—It is you, my mother.

THOMAS CARLYLE

A Mother's love endures through all; in good repute, in bad repute, in the face of the world's condemnation, a mother still loves on.

WASHINGTON IRVING

If I were hanged on the highest hill,
O Mother o' mine, O Mother o' mine!
I know whose love would follow me still,
Mother o' mine, O Mother o' mine.

RUDYARD KIPLING

Into the ward of the clean, white-wash'd halls
Where the dead slept and the dying lay;
Wounded by bayonets, sabres and balls,
Sombody's darling was borne one day.

Somebody's darling, so young and so brave,
Wearing still on his sweet, yet pale face,
Soon to be hid in the dust of the grave,
The lingering light of his boyhood's grace.

Somebody's darling,
Somebody's pride.
Who'll tell his mother
  where her boy died?

                  MARIE REVENEL DE LA COSTE

*J*ust break the news to mother,
She knows how dear I love her,
And tell her not to wait for me,
For I'm not coming home;
Just say there is no other
Can take the place of mother;
Then kiss her dear, sweet lips for me,
And break the news to her.

                      CHAS. K. HARRIS

*F*old up the banners! Smelt the guns!
Love rules. Her gentle purpose runs;
A mighty mother turns in tears
The pages of her battle years,
Lamenting all her fallen sons!

                WILL HENRY THOMPSON

*N*ot for the star-crowned heroes, the
  men that conquer and slay,
But a song for those that bore them, the
  mothers braver than they.
With never a blare of trumpets, with
  never a surge of cheers
They march to the unseen hazard—
  pale, patient volunteers.

          MARK ANTONY DE WOLFE HOWE

*T*he mothers of brave men must themselves be brave.

MARY BALL WASHINGTON, mother
of George Washington

A s I approached the door about nine o'clock in the evening, I heard my mother engaged in prayer. During her prayer she referred to me, her son away God only knew where, and asked that he might be preserved in health to return and comfort her in her old age. At the conclusion of the prayer I quietly raised the latch and entered. I will not attempt to describe the scene that followed. . . .

PRESIDENT JAMES GARFIELD, describing
his return from a youthful job as a canal bargeman

I do know that other things on the face of this earth that have children—mother elephants, robin redbreasts, and so on—*leave* them. Mothers are the only ones that allow their children to keep coming back.

BILL COSBY

M other, mother, pin a rose on me.
Mother, mother, pin a rose on me.
I was quite afraid some spooney girl
Would pin a rose on me.

DAVE LEWIS,
PAUL SCHINDLER, and BOB ADAMS

*D*aughter, don't get married,
Else you will be sorry.
You are much too young, dear.
Marriage brings great worry.
When a girl is married young,
Soon her passing bell is rung.

What is that you're saying?
Young girls can't get married!
Take me to the graveyard,
Show me where they're buried,
Girls who married all too young,
Girls whose passing-bells have rung!

RUMANIAN FOLK SONG

J want a girl, just like the girl
that married dear old Dad.

HARRY VON TILZER

J am training Jane to be a poor man's wife. I want
her to know all the things a girl who marries a
man making a modest salary, say, forty dollars a
week, should and must know.

MRS. A. WITHERS, mother of
child star Jane Withers

"*F*ind work, my daughter, you can milk a cow,
Find work, my daughter, you can milk a cow."
"No, no, my mother, let me marry now.
No, no, my mother, let me marry now."

"Well, then, my daughter, choose a steady man."
"Mother, I want a proper gentleman."

"Daughter, a farmer's better than a king."
"Give me a husband who can dance and sing."

"Find one who'll harrow, dig and rake and grub."
"No, no, my mother, we shall keep a pub."

"O my poor daughter, hungry will you be,
Five sous for white wine, red wine only three."

FRENCH FOLK SONG

A modern mother is one who worries if her daughter gets in too early.

ANONYMOUS

I want Melissa's encounters to be wonderfully romantic, meaningful affairs, not one-night stands. I had my own affairs in the sixties, but it was always done with the courting game, the flowers and romance. When you finally went to bed with somebody, it meant something. . . . Also, I want Melissa to be careful and discreet. And I'm all for marriage.

JOAN RIVERS, on her hopes
for her daughter

*F*or mothers, sons are harder to let go of than daughters.

CAROLYN GARRIS

$\mathcal{T}$he empty nest, as I was led to believe, was going to be a time of boredom and depression. No one told me that it really means having the phone ring and it's for you. It's having leftovers in the refrigerator that you can count on. It's having hot water in the shower, ice cubes in the freezer, gas in your car. It's like being reborn.

ERMA BOMBECK

$\mathcal{Y}$ou know you're still a mother when you spend your days picking up from one room and putting their things in another.

JULIE ANDREWS, on her adult daughters

$\mathcal{T}$hy mother's lot, my dear,
    She doth it naught accuse:
Her lot to bear, to nurse, to rear,
    To love—and then to lose.

JEAN INGELOW

$\mathcal{H}$ is mother from the window look'd,
With all the longing of a mother.

JAMES LOGAN

$\mathcal{T}$he best friend of a boy is his mother, of a man his horse; only it's not clear when the transition takes place.

ANONYMOUS

$\mathcal{M}$y heart, my arms, my mind will always be open to my children. Though I would do anything at all for them, it is they who must live their lives.

ELIZABETH TAYLOR

*R*emember when you were a little boy and you cried because you couldn't have some toy and I told you we were saving all our money for you when you were older? Well, dear, I was lying.

MARY CHASE

*H*e that would the daughter win
Must with the mother first begin.

JOHN RAY

*W*hen a young woman behaves to her parents in a manner particularly tender and respectful, I mean from principle as well as nature, there is nothing good and gentle that may not be expected from her in whatever condition she is placed. Of this I am so thoroughly persuaded, that, were I to advise any friend of mine as to his choice of a wife, I know not whether my first counsel would not be, "Look out for one distinguished by her attention and sweetness to her parents."

DAVID FORDYCE

A lot of men tell their women how different the women are from Mother. This part of the conversation can be safely ignored. It is best to assume that you are a variant or a slightly improved model of the mother, or else he would not be going out with you at all.

JOHN LEO

𝒥 love Ava. She's a grand girl and naturally I want Mickey to be happy. But I give the marriage three weeks before it's over.

MRS. NELL PANKEY, on
her son Mickey Rooney's
marriage to Ava Gardner

𝓔 very bride has to learn it's not her wedding but her mother's.

LUCI JOHNSON NUGENT

𝒥f all mothers want to be demanding or irrational before their children's weddings, I suppose it is their right.

VANESSA L. OCHS

𝒫 robably there is nothing in human nature more resonant with charges than the flow of energy between two biologically alike bodies, one of which has lain in amniotic bliss inside the other, one of which has labored to give birth to the other.

ADRIENNE RICH

𝒯 hou art thy mother's glass, and she in thee
Calls back the lovely April of her prime.

WILLIAM SHAKESPEARE

s is the mother, so is her daughter.

EZEKIEL 16:44

he awe and dread with which the untutored savage contemplates his mother-in-law are among the most familiar facts of anthropology.

SIR GEORGE FRAZIER

 nd Ruth said, Intreat me not to leave thee, or to return from following after thee: for whither thou goest, I will go; and where thou lodgest I will lodge; thy people shall be my people, and thy God, my God. Where thou diest, will I die, and there will I be buried: the Lord do so to me, and more also, if ought but death part thee and me.

RUTH 1:16–17 to her
mother-in-law, Naomi

 he was to me all that a mother could be, and I yield to none in admiration for her character, love of her virtues, and veneration for her memory.

ROBERT E. LEE, on his mother-
in-law, Mary Custis

 owever much you dislike your mother-in-law, you must not set fire to her.

ERNEST WILD (recorder of London),
addressing a felon brought
before him in 1925

ℬecause I feel that, in the Heavens above,
  The angels, whispering to one another,
Can find, among their burning terms of love,
  None so devotional as that of "Mother,"
Therefore by that dear name I long have called you—
  You who are more than mother unto me.
And fill my heart of hearts, where death installed
  you
  In setting my Virginia's spirit free.
My mother—my own mother, who died early,
  Was but the mother of myself; but you
Are mother to the one I loved so dearly,
  And thus are dearer than the mother I knew
By that infinity with which my wife
  Was dearer to my soul than it's soul-life.

EDGAR ALLAN POE

ℬe civil to a mother-in-law and she will come to
your house three times a day.

JAPANESE PROVERB

𝒜 mother, asked if she had yet made the long trip
across the country to visit her son and his new
wife, replied: "No, I've been waiting until they
have their first baby."

"You don't want to spend the money for the trip
until then?"

"No," the wise lady explained. "It's just that I
have a theory grandmas are more welcome than
mothers-in-law."

WALL STREET JOURNAL

$\mathcal{B}$ecoming a grandparent is a second chance. For you have a chance to put to use all the things you learned the first time around and may have made a mistake on. It's all love and no discipline. There's no thorn in this rose.

DR. JOYCE BROTHERS

$\mathcal{I}$'m not a picture-toting grandma—but my grandsons, Tyler J. Phillips and Dean Phillips, just happen to be the best-looking, smartest, best-mannered grandchildren in the continental United States— and you can throw in Canada and the Virgin Islands.

ABIGAIL VAN BUREN

$\mathcal{I}$f mothers perfect any talent during their tenure as mothers, it is the ability to worry well. With ten children, I have become a professional worrier, a fact which panics my husband since he read someplace that "worriers tend to die younger than nonworriers." This, of course, is nonsense. If that were true, there wouldn't be any living grandmothers. None of them would have survived as mothers.

THERESA BLOOMINGDALE

$\mathcal{I}$ remember the time I realized I didn't come first with anybody in this world anymore. My children had children who had children who must take top spot. They had husbands and wives of their own. I had no husband to come first *to*. Then I realized I had a lot of seconds and thirds, and these add up.

ADELA ROGERS ST.-JOHN

*G*ranny was so important to my life, but for most children she isn't even around. That's a loss. It's the loss of an understanding ear and of a person who has much love to give but a love that is not bounded by expectation. It's not Granny's fault if you are not perfect. But parents feel it is their fault if their children do not achieve. Children sense that. I know my own grandchildren tell me things they could not tell their parents.

CHASE GOING WOODHOUSE

I never thought she'd turn on me. When I was sinking in a sea of diapers, formulas and congenital spitting, Mother couldn't wait to pull her grandchildren onto her lap and say, "Let me tell you how rotten your mommy was. She never took naps, and she never picked up her room, and she had a mouth like a drunken sailor in Shanghai. I washed her mouth out with soap so many times I finally had to starch her tongue."

ERMA BOMBECK

*T*he dining table has a vinyl cloth
we're using paper napakins.
My husband just doesn't keep house
according to my mother's standards.

NATASHA JOSEFOWITZ

PART V
The Mother of Success

Men are what their mothers made them.
RALPH WALDO EMERSON

$\mathcal{I}$ expect my children to be like me, only better.

ANGELA BARRON MCBRIDE

$\mathcal{M}$y mother was already laying plans for a long hard struggle to come up from the bottom, and I was central to them. I would "make something" of myself, and if I lacked the grit to do it, well, then she would make me make something of myself. I would become the proof of the strength of her womanhood.

RUSSELL BAKER

$\mathcal{I}$ knew myself destined to reach those dizzy heights so clearly visible to my mother's eyes. In the darkest moments of the war, in the thick of battle, I always faced peril with a feeling of invincibility. Nothing could happen to me because I was her happy ending.

ROMAIN GARY

$\mathcal{D}$on't aim to be an earthly saint, with eyes
    fixed on a star,
Just try to be the fellow that your Mother
    thinks you are.

WILL S. ADKIN

$\mathcal{S}$it in the seat of thy mother
And walk in thy mother's footsteps.

JOHANN GOTTFRIED VON HERDER

$\mathcal{M}$aybe Mom is my alter ego and the woman I'm
able to be when I'm working.

MARY TYLER MOORE

$\mathcal{S}$he's my teacher, my adviser, my greatest inspiration.

WHITNEY HOUSTON

$\mathcal{I}$n loving memory of my
    MOTHER
without whom I might have been
    somebody else.

MAE WEST, the dedication of
her autobiography

$\mathcal{I}$ have been perfectly happy the way I am. If my
mother was responsible for it, I am grateful.

CHRISTOPHER ISHERWOOD

$\mathcal{W}$ith a mother of a different caliber, I should
probably have turned out badly. But her firmness,

her sweetness, her goodness, were potent powers to keep me on the right path.

THOMAS ALVA EDISON

His mother's kindness is a debt,
He never, never will forget.

JANE TAYLOR

In the man whose childhood has known caresses and kindness, there is always a fiber of memory that can be touched to gentle issues.

GEORGE ELIOT

Yet, dearest mother, such the gentle worth
Of thy benignant presence, angel-mild,
It ever hath my proudest moods beguiled,
And given to softer, humbler feelings birth.

HEINRICH HEINE

What are Raphael's Madonnas but the shadow of a mother's love, fixed in permanent outline forever?

THOMAS WENTWORTH HIGGINSON

All that I am, my mother made me.

JOHN QUINCY ADAMS

A mother is not a person to lean on but a person to make leaning unnecessary.

DOROTHY CANFIELD FISHER

*T*he character of the son begins to develop when he hears his mother complain that her husband has no place in the government, of which the consequence is that she has no precedence among other women.

PLATO

*M*others all want their sons to grow up to be president but they don't want them to become politicians in the process!

JOHN F. KENNEDY

*J*immy says he'll never tell a lie. Well, I lie all the time. I have to—to balance the family ticket.

LILLIAN CARTER

*C*ongressmen, all of whom have mothers, know how sensitive this class of woman can become when the institution of motherhood is slighted. Congressmen also have an especially soft spot in their hearts for mothers, for they know that mothers are so humane they will forgive their children anything, even the fact that they sometimes become Congressmen.

RUSSELL BAKER

*B*ehind every successful man stands a surprised mother-in-law.

HUBERT HUMPHREY

*W*ell, I don't know anything about politics, and I don't know whether Tom will make a good president. But I'll tell you one thing: he's a lousy poker player.

> ANNIE LOUISE DEWEY,
> shortly before the 1948
> election which her son Thomas was
> expected to win easily

I certainly did, and I am thinking of voting again on my way home.

> MARTHA ELLEN TRUMAN, Harry's
> mother, when asked on election day,
> 1948, if she had voted yet

*T*he President of India died, and I called Mama to ask her to represent me there. When she answered the phone I asked her what she was doing. She said she was sitting around the house looking for something to do, and I said, "How would you like to go to India?" She said, "I'd love to go someday. Why?" I said, "How about this afternoon?" She said, "Okay, I'll be ready."

[This diary excerpt for February 11, 1977, is followed by this comment:]

On occasion, my mother, Lillian, was eagerly accepted as the official representative our country and its President, especially in communities where advanced age is revered, liberal social views are appreciated, and a lively sense of humor is tolerated.

> JIMMY CARTER

*T*his is a moment I deeply wish my parents could have lived to share. In the first place my father would have enjoyed what you have so generously said of me—and my mother would have believed it.

LYNDON B. JOHNSON

*M*y mother—her name is Rose Szolnoki now— raised me and she had her hands full. I think she did a helluva job. She taught me to be polite and to respect my elders. She's a great lady, and she loves to talk. She talks very slowly and very properly. We have a running gag among my friends that whenever my mother calls on the phone she uses up the first three minutes just to say hello. And she does some of the funniest things in the world. When she watches the Jets play on television, she prays to two saints, one when we've got the ball and one when the other team's got the ball. She's the only person I know who has an offensive saint and a defensive saint.

JOE NAMATH

I know what a superstar she is by the reaction I get when I tell people Patti Labelle is my mother. First it's disbelief, then, "Can you get me an autograph?" But at home, she's just mom—always in the kitchen cleaning up or cooking something new.

STANLEY EDWARDS, Patti Labelle's adopted son

*M*y mother's cooking was heroic. That means she had no particular love, no particular talent, but an extraordinary desire to be a good wife and mother.

ROBERT PRITSKER

*I*t makes me very happy, and I think it's a lovely compliment to Mother, that she has become so internationally known that no matter where I go the first question I'm asked by famous personages such as the Queen of England and her mother, the President of the United States, governors, and mayors is, "How's your dear mother?"

LIBERACE

*A*s Mother has said so often, "Remember, wherever you are and whatever you do, someone always sees you."

MARIAN ANDERSON

I was there with my mother every time she pawned her diamond ring and gold bracelet—and we worried together that Daddy would notice they were gone. I'd get terrified—so many experiences of my mother being told in Saks Fifth Avenue, "They want to speak to you upstairs." . . . To this day, I'll give my MasterCharge and hold my breath.

JOAN RIVERS

*M*y mother is a strong-minded woman, but she was never a "stage mama." During those vaudeville years, my sisters and I, while standing in countless wings waiting for our cues, used to hear other mothers threatening their children, saying things like, "You go on out there or I'll break your head," and it made us kind of sick. Nobody ever talked to me like that or forced me in any way. I drove myself—but it was my own doing.

JUDY GARLAND

I had one special thing to get rid of. I had to bury my mother. At last. I had never had the time—or taken the time—to mourn her or to really bury her, that sort of burial that doesn't take place in the ground but in the spirit. My mother is dead—a fact that a lot of people may not like, but it's true. I wasn't allowed the normal grieving process. I went through it now, fifteen years after her funeral. There's a danger in keeping somebody who's dead alive in your mind. I had been very good at that. When you bury somebody, you stop justifying, defending and thinking about them all the time. A burden was lifted. . . . I was overprotective. I saw myself as my mother's mother. What I didn't know was that I loved her too much. Now, at last, I understand.

LIZA MINNELLI

I had chosen my parents with care. Totally different in character and mentality, they offered a wide choice of guidelines, and I helped myself. My father was serious, reserved, meticulous to a fault, sometimes explosive, always impatient. My mother was serene, forgetful, communicative, and tolerant. I took after my father, both outwardly and inwardly. Which is probably why I loved my mother at first sight. Just as he did.

LILI PALMER

One may desert one's father, though he be a high official, but not one's mother, though she be a beggar.

CHINESE PROVERB

I want to talk about my mother—I mean the heart, body and soul of my mother—because I believe my mother is one of God's greatest creations. I want to talk about the anatomy of my mother—her hands, her feet, and her knees, because those parts are all so very special to me. It was her feet that carried her across town to do domestic work for the white folks: and once at those white folks' houses, my mother had to get down on her hands and knees to scrub floors, scrub toilets and wash dirty, stinky diapers.

MR. T.

A noble mother must have bred
So brave a son.

GEORGE CAMPBELL

Women are naturally superior; they're our only hope. I mean, my mother lives with me.

LARRY FLYNT, publisher of *Hustler*

H appy he
With such a mother! faith in womankind
Beats with his blood, and trust in all things high
Comes easy to him; and tho' he trip and fall
He shall not bind his soul with clay.

ALFRED, LORD TENNYSON

O ur children were our hobby, our main activity.
We both spent a lot of time with them. We didn't
do it out of duty; we really enjoyed it. Little
League, Cub Scouts, Boy Scouts, the works. From
the time they were little, I had structured a time
for each child. It was their individual session with
me. Even if it was only fifteen minutes—and generally it was more, up to about an hour—that
time was theirs, and nothing could interfere. We
might color, talk, or just curl up together. You
couldn't cheat, like "Mommy is going to hold you
while she makes phone calls." I remember coloring with Jeff, and Beau would say, "Can't I color,
too?" And he would have to understand that it
was not his time.

DOROTHY (MRS. LLOYD) BRIDGES

S he was really the guiding force of my entering
the ballet. I entered in a very insane manner. I
was knocked unconscious by a baseball while she
was taking my older sister to a local dance school
in Bayside. When she found out what happened to
me when she wasn't home, she dragged me along
to the ballet school with them.

EDWARD VILLELLA

𝓜en are what their mothers make them.

EDWARD BULWER-LYTTON

𝓜y earliest memories were of my mother writing her PhD dissertation and taking care of my brother and myself. Her emphasis on education, social responsibility, and the importance of a woman's fulfilling herself have shaped my outlook fundamentally and irrevocably.

REPRESENTATIVE ELIZABETH HOLTZMAN

𝓜other was a Phi Beta Kappa and a psychology graduate of the University of California. In those days women who were scholars were viewed with some suspicion. When Mother and Dad were married, the Oakland paper said:

"Although a graduate of the University of California, the bride is nonetheless an extremely attractive young woman."

Indeed she was.

FRANK B. GILBRETH, JR., and
ERNESTINE GILBRETH CAREY

𝓘 wanted to do something she could be proud of me for—I come from a large family, so I thought it would mean a lot if I could go to college and set an example for the other kids.

WALT FRAZIER

O, 'tis a parlous boy;
Bold, quick, ingenious, forward, capable;
He is all the mother's, from top to toe.

WILLIAM SHAKESPEARE

*D*id I ever tell you of an occasion when Whistler let me see him with the paint off—with his brave mask down? Once standing by me in his studio— Tite Street—we were looking at the "Mother." I said some string of words about the beauty of the face and figure—and for some moments Jimmy looked and looked, but he said nothing. His hand was playing with that tuft on his nether lip. It was perhaps two minutes before he spoke. "Yes," very slowly, and very softly—"yes—one does like to make one's mummy just as nice as possible."

HARPER PENNINGTON

*I*t is the general rule that all superior men inherit the elements of their superiority from their mothers.

JULES MICHELET

*S*he was an exceptional woman! Just think of what she did in Madrid: she studied foreign languages and more or less did the same lessons as I did, partly because she thought it would help me with my work, but mostly because the deep feeling we had for each other should not be affected by any differences in our education.

PABLO CASALS

ℱor me, the most personal thing I ever said on the air had to do with my mother, who had recently died. I said that she'd wanted to go to college but there was no money, that she'd wanted to work but her husband wouldn't let her, that she'd wanted to go into politics but she knew no other women in politics. She'd said it wasn't her time. Instead, she'd pushed me to read, to stretch, even when she didn't agree with what I read or where I stretched. She said it was my time, and so I pointed out on the air that this two minutes at the end of a television show was indeed my time and I wanted to use it to say a public and sincere thank you, from my time to hers, from me to her.

LINDA ELLERBEE

𝒮he was very proud of my being a published writer, and we generally shared the same values. After her death, I found a mother-daughter morals quiz I once had written for a women's magazine. In her unmistakably shaky writing, she had recorded her own answers, her entirely accurate imagination of what my answers would be, and a score that concluded her differences were less than those "normal for women separated by twenty-odd years."

GLORIA STEINEM

𝒲hile my father endowed me with my ravishing good looks and stubbornness, it was through my mother's genes that I received my passionate love of books. But she was never able to indulge fully in that love because she grew up in Mississippi and she wasn't allowed into the public libraries. And so she worked in the fields in her spare afternoons to get the extra money to send away to book clubs. . . . Realizing that I was a painfully shy child, she gave me my first diary and told me to write my feelings down in there. Over the years that diary was followed by reams and reams of paper that eventually culminated into *The Women of Brewster Place*. And I wrote that book as a tribute to her and other black women who, in spite of very limited personal circumstances, somehow manage to hold fierce belief in the limitless possibilities of the human spirit. And since you've chosen to honor it tonight, she thanks you.

> GLORIA NAYLOR, accepting the
> American Book Award for a
> first novel in 1983

*A*s more and more mothers of achievement come to light, they may in time relegate the fathers to equality, a status they may possibly prefer to one that has become a cliché. After all, although the thought is father to the deed, we have known for centuries that necessity is the mother of invention.

> ROSE ORENTE

PART VI
Enduring Ties

Youth fades; love droops; the leaves of friendship fall; A mother's secret love outlives them all.

OLIVER WENDELL HOLMES

𝓔very man is privileged to believe all his life that his own mother is the best and dearest that a child ever had. By some strange racial instinct of taciturnity and repression most of us lack utterance to say our thoughts in this close matter. A man's mother is so tissued and woven into his life and brain that he can no more describe her than describe the air and sunlight that bless his days.

CHRISTOPHER MORLEY

𝒯he mother's love—there's none so pure,
  So constant and so kind;
No human passion doth endure
  Like this within the mind.

ANONYMOUS

𝒯he older I become, the more I think about my mother.

INGMAR BERGMAN

𝓜other, do you know, almost all people love their mothers, but I have never met anybody in my life, I think, who loved his mother as much as I love you. . . . I was telling somebody yesterday that the reason I am a poet is entirely because you wanted me to be and intended I should be, even from the very first. . . . I cannot remember once in my life when you were not interested in what I was working on, or even suggested that I should put it aside for something else. Some parents of children that are "different" have so much to reproach themselves with. But not you, Great Spirit. . . .

If I didn't keep calling you mother, anybody reading this would think I was writing to my sweetheart. And he would he be quite right.

EDNA ST. VINCENT MILLAY

To my first Love, my Mother, on whose
    knee
I learnt love-lore that is not troublesome;
    Whose service is my special dignity,
And she my lodestar while I come and go.

CHRISTINA G. ROSSETTI

Her heart is like her garden,
    Old-fashioned, quaint and sweet,
With here a wealth of blossoms,
    And there a still retreat.

ALICE E. ALLEN

I look into my inmost mind
And here her inspiration find.

JOSEPHINE RICE CREELMAN

𝓐 woman is her mother.

ANNE SEXTON

𝒲e are right to expect more from life, to demand more as people demand more of us. But our mothers are right too in reminding us that life is not always what it seems, that what looks good today may turn on us tomorrow, that what comes to us camouflaged as a brave new order may still be the same old story. It is not that our mothers are resistant to change—it is just that they've lived through enough to know change is fleeting and hard-won.

ROSEMARY L. BRAY

𝓘 spent hours rummaging through my mother's drawers, dabbing her cologne behind my ears, putting on her rhinestone earrings, reading anniversary cards my father had given her, sifting through the hodgepodge in her pocketbooks. I was hunting for clues about what it was to be a woman. I was searching for some secret I knew she had, but wouldn't willingly share with me.

ANGELA BARRON MCBRIDE

𝒮tored atop the closet shelf of my old bedroom in my parents' house are half a dozen diaries. I began writing them at age twelve for the express purpose of insuring that I didn't commit the same outrages against my children that my mother was busy committing against me. All her crimes are well documented in their pages. . . .

I can hope that I will have an endless supply of empathy for my son, but at times I'm sure that, like my mother, I'll have good intentions. I'm also sure that my son will keep his own diary, whatever form it takes—and I hope that someday, when he sees parenthood from the inside out, he'll find within himself the same spirit of healing rising within me now.

ROBERTA ISRAELOFF

M y mother won't admit it, but I've always been a disappointment to her. Deep down inside, she'll never forgive herself for giving birth to a daughter who refuses to launder aluminum foil and use it over again.

ERMA BOMBECK

O nce we have given birth to a child we have undertaken a life-long calling. To conceive of it in any other way is to delude ourselves. My parents still worry about their forty-four-year-old son who homesteads alone in Alaska.

JAIN SHERRARD

I am not the best person in the world; there are things about me that I would change if I could, and that I would not particularly respect if I found them in other people. But I know this: whenever I am doing something I sense might be wrong, I can check myself out by asking myself whether I would be ashamed if my mother knew about it.

BOB GREENE

No language can express the power and beauty and heroism and majesty of a mother's love. It shrinks not where man cowers, and grows stronger where man faints, and over the wastes of worldly fortune sends the radiance of quenchless fidelity like a star in heaven.

E. H. CHAPIN

She is the sweet rallying-point of affection, obedience, and a thousand tendernesses.

LAMARTINE

But I had not so much of man in me,
And all my mother came into mine eyes
And gave me up to tears.

WILLIAM SHAKESPEARE

St. Leon raised his kindling eye,
And lifts the sparkling cup on high;
    "I drink to one," he said,
"Whose image never may depart,
Deep graven on this grateful heart,
    Till memory be dead. . . ."
St. Leon paused, as if he would
Not breathe her name in careless mood,
    Thus lightly to another;
Then bent his noble head, as though
To give that word the reverence due,
    And gently said: "My Mother!"

THE KNIGHT'S TOAST, author
unknown, sometimes attributed
to Sir Walter Scott

*A*nd now so well I know her that I know
The graciousness of her will always grow
Like daybreak in my spirit, and will be
Through all my life a radiant mystery
Since love like hers ever exceeds the sweep
Of mortal plummet, sound we ne'er so deep.

AMELIA JOSEPHINE BURR

*O*h! there is an enduring tenderness in the love of
a mother to a son that transcends all other affec-
tions of the heart. It is neither to be chilled by
selfishness, nor daunted by danger, nor weakened
by worthlessness, nor stifled by ingratitude. She
will sacrifice every comfort to his convenience;
she will surrender every pleasure to his enjoy-
ment; she will glory in his fame, and exult in his
prosperity; and if adversity overtake him, he will
be the dearer to her by misfortune; and if disgrace
settle upon his name, she will still love and cher-
ish him; and if all the world beside cast him off,
she will be all the world to him.

WASHINGTON IRVING

I love all my children, but some of them I don't like.

LILLIAN CARTER

*T*he end of another busy day brought me a letter
from you. Your letters always give me more
strength, renewed courage, and that bulldog te-
nacity so essential to the success of any man.

LYNDON JOHNSON, in a letter to
his mother, Rebekah

To me your election not only gratifies my pride as a mother in a splendid and satisfying son and delights me with the realization of the joy that you must feel in your success, but it in a measure compensates for the heartache and disappointment I experienced as a child when my dear father lost the race you just won.

REBEKAH BAINES JOHNSON, in a
letter to Lyndon after he won
his first race for Congress

Michael Dearest—I hope this valentine gets to you on your birthday even though it will say what I've said to you so many times before and yet becomes increasingly true. You were not so handsome when I first saw you—forty-two years ago, on the 21st of January—as you are today. But you had something and it took hold of me and has never let go. I could sell that line for a lyric, but I give it to you freely—Happy birthday. Love always, Mother.

P.S. And in case you're asking, where's the gift? Let me remind you, kind hearts are more than coronets.

MARY CHASE, in a
letter to her son Michael

One day at Antibes in 1923, Picasso's mother was introduced to Gertrude Stein. . . . Miss Stein extolled [the painter's] handsomeness when she first met him in 1905, only to be told, "It was nothing compared to his looks when he was a boy. He was an angel and a devil in beauty; no one could cease looking at him."

PIERRE CABANNE

A man who has been the indisputable favorite of his mother keeps for life the feeling of a conqueror, that confidence of success which frequently induces real success.

SIGMUND FREUD

M y dear mother with the truthfulness of a mother's heart, ministered to all my woes, outward and inward, and even against hope kept prophesying good.

THOMAS CARLYLE

W hile plodding on our way, the toilsome road of
   life,
   How few the friends that daily there we meet!
Not many will stand by in trouble and in strife,
   With counsel and affection ever sweet!
But there is one whose smile, will ever on us
   beam,
   Whose love is dearer far than any other
And wherever we may turn,
This lesson we will learn,
   A boy's best friend in his Mother.

      Then cherish her with care,
      And smooth her silv'ry hair,
      When gone you will never get another.

And wherever we may turn,
This lesson we shall learn
A boy's best friend is his Mother.

JOSEPH P. SKELLY

A man outwearied with the world's mad race
his mother seeks again.

IRVING BROWNE

M ammy, Mammy,
The sun shines East, the sun shines West,
But I've just learned where the sun shines best,
Mammy, Mammy,
My heart strings are tangled around Alabammy
I'se a'comin', sorry I made you wait;
I'se a'comin', hope and pray I'm not too late.
Mammy, Mammy,
I'd walk a million miles for one of your smiles.
My Mammy.

SAM LEWIS, JOE YOUNG, and
WALTER DONALDSON

H e has been very thoughtful to me. Occasionally
he ignores me and I call him down. He says,
"Mother I don't have to prove my love to you.
Thank goodness you're the one person I don't
have to prove it to."

LILLIAN CARTER, on her son
President Jimmy Carter

*O*h take me to my kind old mudder!
Dere let me live and die.

STEPHEN COLLINS FOSTER

*T*his heart, my own dear mother, bends
With love's true instinct, back to thee!

THOMAS MOORE

*T*he song of the mothers! in infancy our lullaby;
in youth our high clear call to straightness of life;
in age our oftenest rehearsed refrain.

W. J. CAMERON

I would weave you a song, my mother,
Yours the tender hand Upon my breast;
Yours the voice Sounding ever in my ears.

MADELEINE MASON-MANHEIM

*M*y mother used to say, "Some comedy is tragedy plus time."

CAROL BURNETT

*Y*ears to a mother bring distress,
But do not make her love the less.

WILLIAM WORDSWORTH

*M*other—that was the bank where we deposited
all our hurts and worries.

T. DEWITT TALMAGE

*B*ury thy sorrows, and they shall rise
As souls to the immortal skies,
And there look down like mothers's eyes.

GEORGE MEREDITH

*M*other, thou sole and only, thou not these,
Keep me in mind a little when I die,
Because I was thy first born.

ALGERNON CHARLES SWINBURNE

*O*h, when a mother meets on high
  The babe she lost in infancy,
Hath she not there for pains and fears.
  The day of woe, the watchful night,
For all her sorrow, all her tears,
  An overpayment of delight.

ROBERT SOUTHEY

*P*eggy died the morning of November 6, 1915.

The joy in the fullness of life went out of it then and has never quite returned. Deep in the hidden realm of my consciousness my little girl has continued to live, and in that strange, mysterious place where reality and imagination meet, she has grown up to womanhood. There she leads an ideal existence untouched by harsh actuality and disillusion.

Men and women from all classes, from nearly every city in America, poured upon me their sympathy. . . . Women wrote of children dead a quarter of a century for whom they were still secretly mourning, and sent me pictures and locks of hair of their own dead babies. I had never fully realized until then that the loss of a child remains unforgotten to every mother during her lifetime.

MARGARET SANGER

𝒯he only ghosts, I believe, who creep into this world, are dead young mothers, returned to see how their children fare. There is no other inducement great enough to bring the departed back.

SIR JAMES BARRIE

𝒯hou art a widow; yet thou art a mother
And hast the comfort of thy children left thee.

WILLIAM SHAKESPEARE

𝒢rief fills the room of my absent child,
Lies in his bed, walks up and down with me;
Puts on his pretty looks, repeats his words;
Remembers me of all his gracious parts,
Stuffs out his vacant garments with his form;
Then have I reason to be fond of grief.
O Lord, my boy, my Arthur, my fair son!
My life, my joy, my food, my all the world!
My Widow-comfort, and my sorrows' cure.

WILLIAM SHAKESPEARE

𝒮he was like the embodiment of all women who have felt an astonished protest because their children died before them.

REBECCA WEST, describing the
Dowager Queen Mary at the
bier of her son, George VI

You, my son,
Have shown me God.
Your kiss upon my cheek
Has made me feel the gentle touch
Of Him who leads us on.
The memory of your smile, when young,
Reveals His face,
As mellowing years come on apace.
And when you went before,
You left the Gates of Heaven ajar
That I might glimpse,
Approaching from afar,
The glories of His Grace.
Hold, Son, my hand,
Guide me along the path,
That, coming,
I may stumble not,
Nor roam,
Nor fail to show the way
Which leads us—Home.

GRACE GOODHUE COOLIDGE, written five
years after the death of her son, Calvin Jr.

Sometimes when people casually ask where my
daughter is, unblinkingly I answer, "In heaven."
Which is true enough. She is. But, while I believe
that she passed from death to life in the twinkling
of an eye, it is still true that death was the
price of the journey. There is no escaping the
pure pain of that fact, and I've found it's better
not to try.

NIKKI GRIMES

𝒩ot a week passes (perhaps I might with equal veracity say a day) in which I do not think of her. Such was the impression her tenderness made upon me, though the opportunity she had for showing it was so short.

WILLIAM COWPER, whose mother
died when he was six

𝒯he desolation and terror of, for the first time, realizing that the mother can lose you, or you her, and your own abysmal loneliness and helplessness without her.

FRANCIS THOMPSON

ℐt was the earliest terror of my childhood that I might loose my mother and it had gone with me all my days.

THOMAS CARLYLE

ℳy mother's name was Rose, Rose Winter Schrift, source of my strength, talent, *chutzpah* and ingenuity, and the lady I clung to no matter how many times I left home or got married. I even fought death for her, unable to accept the fact that anyone or anything would take her away from me. Until finally, in the intensive care ward after her third heart attack, when they were readying for a pacemaker operation, she pulled all the needles out of her arm, looked at me and said, "Baby, it's time you let me go. Don't forget you're an artist. You did it for both of us. Now I have to go join my partner."

SHELLEY WINTERS

$\mathcal{W}$ith her mother an invalid, Mother never sat down. She used to say, "You'll see, I will never lift a spoon or a finger once Grandma is gone." My mother dropped dead at the age of 62. When she dropped dead, knowing her, she could have been having chest pains and not done anything about them. She just didn't have time to deal with things like that. She was immune.

Grandma is now in a nursing home, which I find difficult to accept, since I think Mom literally killed herself to keep this shell of an old woman out of one. Now that is where she is, and we don't have Mom.

I have a cousin who is a nun. At the funeral she said, "Maggie, try not to be angry. Think how much you care about your mother. That is exactly what your mother was doing for her mother. If you can understand how strongly you feel now, that is how strongly she felt about her mother."

MAGGIE PHALAN, in *Mothers
Talking* by Frances Wells Burck

$\mathcal{I}$t was the strangest experience for me. I'd watched Mama suffering terribly those last few weeks, my thoughts filled with death. Then, suddenly, I was confronting the birth of a new life.

> SISSY SPACEK, who discovered
> she was pregnant one day
> after her mother's death

I am very close to my mother. I know it's not fashionable to be, but we always have been. I have a handicapped sister, and to me, women like my mother, who can cope with that and show the sort of love that endures no matter what, are the most admirable people I know. I only hope that my own child feels about me as I feel about my mother.

> BARBARA WALTERS

I am not cheerful like her, but I can say that over the years she has been dying I have lost some of my bitterness. I have come to see more in her death than irony or injustice, though those things are there. She was a woman of character; she had enormous moral strength; and it is as if the moral strength had become physical, had gotten literally into her heart and were keeping it beating, were keeping her lungs pumping air. As if the sheer momentum of her character were sustaining her.

> ANTHONY BRANDT, on his mother's
> battle with Alzheimer's disease

*S*he's always seemed invincible to me. She just kept going forward.

> JULIE NIXON EISENHOWER, on Pat Nixon

The courage that my mother had
   Went with her, and is with her still;
Rock from New England quarried;
   Now granite in a granite hill.

The golden brooch my mother wore
   She left behind for me to wear;
I have no thing I treasure more;
   Yet it is something I could spare.

Oh, if instead she'd left to me
   The thing she took into the grave!—
That courage like a rock, which she
   Has no more need of, and I have.

             EDNA ST. VINCENT MILLAY

PART VII
Final Tributes

The bravest battle that ever was fought;
  Shall I tell you where and when?
On the maps of the world you will find it not;
  It was fought by the mothers of men.

JOAQUIN MILLER

𝒮he's somebody's mother, boys, you know,
For all she's aged and poor and slow.

MARY DOW BRINE

𝒥 love old mothers—mothers with white hair,
And kindly eyes, and lips grown softly sweet
With murmured blessings over sleeping babes.

CHARLES S. ROSS

𝒯he purest thing I know in all earth's holding
Is mother love, her precious child enfolding;
Yet when the mother's footstep feeble groweth,
As sweet the child love then which round her
floweth.

ANONYMOUS

𝒮ure I love the dear silver that shines in your
hair,
And the brow that's all furrowed, and wrinkled
with care
I kiss the dear fingers, so toil-worn for me,
Oh, God bless you and keep you, Mother Machree.

RITA JOHNSON YOUNG

109

$\mathcal{M}$e, let the tender office long engage
To rock the cradle of reposing age;
With lenient arts extend a mother's breath,
Make languor smile, and smooth the bed of death,
Explore the thought, explain the asking eye,
And keep awhile one parent from the sky.

ALEXANDER POPE

$\mathcal{W}$ashington, Nov. 2, 1818— The mail brought me too fatal a confirmation of my apprehensions in a letter from my son John, dated at Boston last Wednesday the 28th of October, informing me that between eleven and one o'clock of that day my mother, beloved and lamented more than language can express, yielded up her pure and gentle spirit to its Creator. She was born on the 11th of November, 1744, and had completed within less than a month of her seventy-fourth year. Had she lived to the age of the Patriarchs, every day of her life would have been filled with clouds of goodness and love. There is not a virtue that can abide in the female heart but it was the ornament of hers.

JOHN QUINCY ADAMS

$\mathcal{N}$ever does one feel so utterly helpless as in trying to speak comfort for great bereavement. Time is the only comforter for the loss of a mother.

JANE WELSH CARLYLE, writing
to her husband following the
death of his mother

[I fell] into an overwhelming abyss of liberty. The very liberty which during my mother's lifetime I had so craved, frightened me. I felt dazed, like a kite whose string had been suddenly cut . . . like a drifting wreck at the mercy of wind and tide.

ANDRE GIDE

Even now when I wake at night
in some room far from everyone,
the darkness sometimes
lightens a little, and then,
because of nothing,
in spite of nothing,
in an imaginary daybreak, I see her,
and for that moment I am still her son
and I am in the holy land.

CALWAY KINNELL

O mother mine! God grant I ne'er forget,
    Whatever be my grief, or what my joy,
The unmeasured, inextinguishable debt
    I owe thy love.

GEORGE W. BETHUNE

Her soul was so luminous, so highly colored, and so warm, that she left a shadow or a chill on nothing.

LAMARTINE

A lady, the loveliest ever the sun
Looked down upon you must paint for me.
Oh, if I could only make you see
The dear blue eyes, the tender smile,
The sovereign's sweetness, the gentle grace,
The woman's soul, and the angel's face
That are beaming on me all the while,
I need not speak these foolish words.
Yet one word tells you all I would say—
She is my mother.

ALICE CORY

Deeply buried within me still lives the happy child, the firstborn son of a youthful mother, who received his first indelible impressions from this air, this soil.

SIGMUND FREUD

Darling Mama. Here with your things before me you are very near. I never showed you in life the love I really felt nor my admiration of your courage and sporting acceptance of illness and losses. Children are cruel things. Forgive me. I had always prayed to show my love by doing something famous for you, to justify what you called me when I got back from France. "My hero son." Perhaps I still may but time grows short. . . .

But you know that I still love you and in the presence of your soul I feel very new and very young and helpless even as I must have been forty-six years ago.

Nothing you ever did to me was anything but loving. I have no other memories of you but love and devotion. It is so sad that we must grow old and separate.

When we meet again I hope you will be lenient for my frailties. In most things I have been worthy.

Perhaps this is foolish but I think you understand.

I loved and love you very much.

Your devoted son.

> GEORGE S. PATTON, JR., in a letter
> written in 1931, three years after his mother's
> death, and left in
> a box of her treasures

The tie which links mother and child is of such pure and immaculate strength as to be never violated, except by those whose feelings are withered by vitiated society. Holy, simple, and beautiful in its construction, it is the emblem of all we can imagine of fidelity and truth; it is the blessed tie whose value we feel in the cradle, and whose loss we lament on the verge of the very grave, where our mother moulders in dust and ashes.

> WASHINGTON IRVING

Well, I guess all of you would say this about your mother. She was a saint.

> RICHARD NIXON

ℐ had but one friend in the world and she is gone.
LORD BYRON, AT HIS MOTHER'S BIER

𝒯he sweetest sounds to mortals given
Are heard in Mother, Home and Heaven.
WILLIAM GOLDSMITH BROWN

𝒯here is a word sweeter than Mother, Home or
Heaven—that word is liberty.
GRAVESTONE of suffragette
Matilda Joslyn Gage

𝒩o earl was ever prouder of his earldom than he
of his descent from a woman who, although well-
born, hesitated not to consecrate to the drama her
brief career of genius and beauty.
EDGAR ALLEN POE, words added
to the gravestone of his mother,
a stage actress, who died when
he was a child

𝒮he had many children of whom only one
had the misfortune to survive her.
THOMAS GRAY, GRAVESTONE OF HIS MOTHER

ℐt is impossible for me to say—to begin to say—
all that has gone down into the grave with her.
She was our life, she was the house, she was the
keystone of the arch. She held us all together, and
without her we are scattered weeds. She was pa-

tience, she was wisdom, she was exquisite maternity. . . . Her death has given me a passionate belief in certain transcendent things—the immanence of being as nobly created as hers—the immortality of such a virtue as that—the reunion of spirits in better conditions than these. She is no more of an angel today than she had always been; but I can't believe that by the accident of her death all her unspeakable tenderness is lost to the beings she so dearly loved. She is with us, she is of us—the eternal stillness is but a form of her love. One can hear her voice in it—one can feel, forever, the inextinguishable vibration of her devotion. . . .

HENRY JAMES

For when you looked into my mother's eyes you knew, as if He had told you, why God sent her into the world—it was to open the minds of all who looked to beautiful thoughts. And that is the beginning and end of literature. Those eyes . . . have guided me through life, and I pray God they may remain my only earthly judge to the last. They were never more my guide than when I helped to put her to earth, not whimpering because my mother had been taken away after seventy-six glorious years of life, but exulting in her even at the grave.

SIR JAMES BARRIE

*W*hat the mother sings to the
cradle goes all the way down
to the grave.

HENRY WARD BEECHER